Praise fo

Asking questions and reciting answers is a method of memorization that has been proven to be successful in passing down legacies of faith. We cannot recommend *A New Baptist Catechism* more highly for parents to instruct their children about the things of God! This updated catechism is relevant to today's issues yet reinforces orthodox theological beliefs that Christians have held for over two centuries. With the scaffolded levels of instruction, *A New Baptist Catechism* can be used by parents with all ages of children too. It is a wonderful resource for families!

—Drs. Jamie and Tara Dew
New Orleans Baptist Theological Seminary

There was a time when Baptists regularly used catechisms to form the hearts and minds of their children. One roadblock to the practice being recovered more widely among Baptists today has been the lack of a simple catechism that uses updated language and addresses topics that are both classical and contemporary. Fortunately, Dwayne Milioni has provided just such a resource with *A New Baptist Catechism*. My prayer is that the Lord will use this resource to help parents to raise their children 'in the discipline and instruction of the Lord' (Ephesians 6:4, ESV).

—Dr. Nathan A. Finn
Provost/Dean of the University Faculty
North Greenville University

A NEW BAPTIST CATECHISM

Important Questions and Answers to Instruct Children About God and the Gospel

Written By
Dwayne Milioni

Seed Publishing Group, LLC
Timmonsville, South Carolina

A New Baptist Catechism:
Important Questions and Answers to
Instruct Children About God and the Gospel

Copyright © 2020 by Dwayne Milioni

Published by:
Seed Publishing Group
2570 Double C Farm Ln
Timmonsville, SC 29161
seed-publishing-group.com

Edited by:
Bill Curtis, Ph.D.

All rights reserved. No part of this book may be reproduced or transmitted in any form or by any means, electronic or mechanical, including photocopying and recording, or by any information storage or retrieval system, except as may be expressly permitted in writing by the publisher. Requests for permission should be addressed in writing to Seed Publishing Group, LLC; 2570 Double C Farm Lane; Timmonsville, SC 29161.

Scripture quotations are from The Holy Bible, English Standard Version® (ESV®), copyright © 2001 by Crossway, a publishing ministry of Good News Publishers.
Used by permission.
All rights reserved.

To order additional copies of this resource visit
www.seed-publishing-group.com.

Library of Congress Control Number: 2020941298

ISBN-13: 978-0-9985451-8-9

Printed in the United States of America

To my children's children. May you grow in the grace and knowledge of our Lord and Savior Jesus Christ.

CONTENTS

Foreword 8

Preface 12

Part One: The Bible 16

Part Two: God 20

Part Three: Jesus Christ 24

Part Four: The Holy Spirit 28

Part Five: Creation and People 32

Part Six: The Fall and Sin 38

Part Seven: God's Holy Law 42

Part Eight: Salvation 50

Part Nine: Prayer 56

Part Ten: The Church 60

Part Eleven: Angels and Demons 66

Part Twelve: Last Things 70

Finding L.I.F.E. in Jesus 76

FOREWORD

Foreword

Catechisms have existed as resources within the church for centuries. The word itself has its roots in a Greek word that means "to resound, with." In other words, catechisms are question and answer books, in which the teacher asks a question, and the student "resounds," or restates, a previously learned answer to the question. In this way, the student practices learning and restating the answers until their truth is deeply internalized. Catechisms for the church are books that teach adults and children foundational Bible doctrines.

One of the earliest Christian catechisms may be found in the New Testament, in 1 Timothy 3:16. One can almost hear a parent ask the question: "How is Jesus a picture of true godliness?" The child replies,

> He appeared in the flesh,
> was vindicated by the Spirit,
> was seen by angels,
> was preached among the nations,
> was believe on in the world,
> was taken up in glory.

There have been several historically significant catechisms for the church since the time of the Reformation. The first was written by Martin Luther, who published his larger and shorter catechisms in 1529. Similarly, in the tradition of John Calvin, the Westminster longer and shorter catechisms are perhaps the best known catechisms of all. Published in 1647, the opening question in the Westminster Shorter Catechism is known the world over:

Foreword

> Teacher: "What is the chief end of man?
>
> Student: "The chief end of man is to glorify God, and to enjoy him forever."

In 1855, Charles Spurgeon published his famous catechism for Baptists. Because Baptists have historically wrestled with the tension between God's Sovereignty and human responsibility in matters of salvation, Spurgeon wanted to write a catechism that reflected that tension. His catechism provided a much needed balance for the Baptist Church.

Over time, there was a diminished use of catechisms by the Baptist Church. In its place, a variety of church programs developed to teach children Bible stories and verses. One of the most famous such programs is AWANA, which many churches, including mine, use to great effect. Yet, these programs do not provide a systematic way to instruct our children in the fundamental doctrines of the Christian faith.

That is why I'm so excited about this book! Now more than ever, our children need to learn the doctrines of our faith. Centuries ago Jude wrote,

> Beloved, although I was very eager to write to you about our common salvation, I found it necessary to write appealing to you to contend for the faith that was once for all delivered to the saints. For certain people have crept in unnoticed who long ago were designated for this condemnation, ungodly people, who pervert the grace of our God into sensuality and deny our only Master and Lord, Jesus Christ (v. 3-4).

Foreword

In many ways, Jude serves as a type of catechism, which warns the Church to resist false teachers through their deep knowledge of the "faith once for all delivered to the saints."

In today's secularized world, our children experience a constant assault on their faith. They will not be able to contend for the faith if the truth of the Gospel is not deeply rooted in their hearts. I want to urge you to purchase this book and teach your children the doctrines it contains. You will be amazed at the amount of theology they will learn. However, this isn't a one-and-done study. It is critically important that you continue to review and reflect upon these doctrines throughout their childhood. In this way, they will be able to achieve the goal that Jude longed to see in his own family and church so long ago:

Now to him who is able to keep you from stumbling and to present you blameless before the presence of his glory with great joy, to the only God, our Savior, through Jesus Christ our Lord, be glory, majesty, dominion, and authority, before all time and now and forever. Amen. (Jude 24-25).

Bill Curtis, Ph.D.
Lead Pastor, Cornerstone Baptist Church

PREFACE

Then children were brought to him that he might lay his hands on them and pray. The disciples rebuked the people, but Jesus said, *"Let the little children come to me and do not hinder them, for to such belongs the kingdom of heaven."* And he laid his hands on them and went away. Matthew 9:13–15 (ESV)

But as for you (Timothy), continue in what you have learned and have firmly believed, knowing from whom you learned it and how from childhood you have been acquainted with the sacred writings, which are able to make you wise for salvation through faith in Christ Jesus. 2 Timothy 3:14–15

What is a Catechism?

A catechism is a tool to instruct children and young believers on Christian beliefs using the form of questions and answers.

Why is this type of instruction important?

Throughout church history, Christians have expressed their beliefs on important doctrines by way of creeds and catechisms. A creed (from the Latin *credo*, "I believe") is a statement of beliefs. A catechism (also a Latin word, meaning "to teach") is an instructional tool used to understand and memorize Bible doctrine.

Creeds and catechisms are not intended to replace Scripture, but to help in understanding it. Baptists have historically held to the sole authority of the Bible (*sola scriptura*) and have used creeds (or confessions) and catechisms to provide insight and instruction on the Bible.

There have been numerous catechisms written since the Reformation. Many Baptist leaders have written catechism for use in their churches. Men such as John Bunyan (1675), Benjamin Keach (1693), Charles Spurgeon (1855), and James P. Boyce (1888) have all provided these effective instructional tools for teachers and parents to train children in their congregations and homes. The use of catechisms remains a powerful tool to help children understand God and his gospel.

How do you use this catechism?

This catechism is for children and new believers to memorize basic, Baptistic Christian doctrine. Much has been gleaned from older catechisms and revised for the contemporary learner. The question and answer format allow a parent or teacher to work systematically through the major areas of theology.

This catechism has been written and illustrated for three types of children: the very young who cannot read; young children who are learning to read; and older children who are reading and have a greater capacity to memorize.

For very young children and those who cannot read there are narrated illustrations for children to enjoy and follow along. For other children, follow these steps:

Step 1: Read the question to the child

Step 2: Read the answer

Step 3: Go back and repeat the question

Step 4: Have the child repeat the answer

Step 5: Repeat the question one more time

Preface

Step 6: Have the child repeat the answer one more time

Step 7: Encourage the child for giving the correct answer

When answering the questions, younger children need only answer the question in **bold font** (shorter answer) while older children should give the complete, two-sentence answer.

Also, there is an optional Bible verse that corresponds to the questions for children to memorize. The verses are important because they show how the answers to the questions are derived from the scriptures. Most of the verses are complete, though some are partial verses for ease of memorization.

PART ONE
THE BIBLE

Part One: The Bible

Question: What is the Bible?

Answer: **The Bible is God's Word**. It is true and trustworthy in everything it says.

All Scripture is breathed out by God and profitable for teaching, for reproof, for correction, and for training in righteousness. 2 Timothy 3:16

Question: Who wrote the Bible?

Answer: **People chosen by God wrote the Bible**. They were guided by the Holy Spirit to write every word.

For no prophecy was ever produced by the will of man, but men spoke from God as they were carried along by the Holy Spirit. 2 Peter 1:21

Question: Why is the Bible important?

Answer: **The Bible teaches me about God and his gospel**. It is the only book that has divine authority.

When you received the word of God, which you heard from us, you accepted it not as the word of men but as what it really is, the word of God, which is at work in you believers. 1 Thessalonians 2:13

Question: How can I get saved?

Answer: **By repenting of my sin and believing the good news about Jesus**. The true gospel is found only in the Bible.

From childhood you have been acquainted with the sacred writings, which are able to make you wise for salvation through faith in Christ Jesus. 2 Timothy 3:15

Question: How can I know God's Word?

Answer: **I know God's Word by reading the Bible.** I should meditate on the scriptures every day.

But his delight is in the law of the Lord, and on his law he meditates day and night.
Psalm 1:2

Question: How can I obey God?

Answer: **The Bible teaches me how to obey.** It is the only book that tells me who God is and what he demands of me.

I have stored up your word in my heart, that I might not sin against you.
Psalm 119:11

PART TWO
GOD

Part Two: God

Question: Who made you?

Answer: **God made me**. I am special because I am made in God's image.

So God created man in his own image, in the image of God he created him; male and female he created them. Genesis 1:27

Question: Why did God make me?

Answer: **God made me to bring him glory.** I am to enjoy God and worship him.

I give thanks to you, O Lord my God, with my whole heart, and I will glorify your name forever. Psalm 86:12

Question: What else did God make?

Answer: **God made everything**. He created the universe for his own praise and glory.

All things were made through him, and without him was not anything made that was made. John 1:3

Question: How can I please God?

Answer: **By loving and obeying him**. I am to love God with all my heart, soul, and strength.

For this is the love of God, that we keep his commandments. And his commandments are not burdensome. 1 John 5:3

Question: Why should I obey God?

Answer: **I should obey God because he loves me**. He always knows what is best for me.

Give thanks to the God of heaven, for his steadfast love endures forever. Psalm 136:26

Question: Is there only one God?

Answer: **Yes, there is only one God.** God alone is worthy of our praise and worship.

Hear, O Israel: The LORD our God, the LORD is one. Deuteronomy 6:4

Question: Is Jesus God too?

Answer: **Yes, Jesus is God and so is the Holy Spirit.** There is one God and he exists in three persons.

In the beginning was the Word, and the Word was with God, and the Word was God. John 1:1

Question: Who is God?

Answer: **God is Spirit.** He is all-powerful and unchangeable.

God is spirit, and those who worship him must worship in spirit and truth. John 4:24

Question: What is God like?

Answer: **God is holy.** He is perfect in goodness, justice, and mercy.

Holy, holy, holy, is the Lord God Almighty, who was and is and is to come! Revelation 4:8

Question: Where is God?

Answer: **God is everywhere all the time.** He is infinite and eternal.

"I am the Alpha and the Omega," says the Lord God, "who is and who was and who is to come, the Almighty." Revelation 1:8

Question: Can you see God?

Answer: **I cannot see God, but he always sees me**. God is invisible and reigns from heaven.

To the King of the ages, immortal, invisible, the only God, be honor and glory forever and ever. Amen. 1 Timothy 1:17

Question: What does God know?

Answer: **God knows everything**. I cannot hide anything from him.

And no creature is hidden from his sight, but all are naked and exposed to the eyes of him to whom we must give account. Hebrews 4:13

Question: What can God do?

Answer: **God can do anything he wants to**. He always does what his perfect will demands.

Ah, Lord God! It is you who have made the heavens and the earth by your great power and by your outstretched arm! Nothing is too hard for you. Jeremiah 32:17

PART THREE
JESUS CHRIST

Part Three: Jesus Christ

Question: Who is Jesus Christ?
Answer: **Jesus Christ is the Son of God**. He is the second person in the Trinity.

And those in the boat worshiped him, saying, "Truly you are the Son of God." Matthew 14:33

Question: Is Jesus God's Son?
Answer: **Yes, God sent his only Son to save us.** Jesus is God in every way.

For God so loved the world, that he gave his only Son, that whoever believes in him should not perish but have eternal life. John 3:16

Question: Is Jesus Mary's Son too?
Answer: **Yes, Jesus was born from the Virgin Mary**. Jesus is human in every way.

Behold, the virgin shall conceive and bear a son, and they shall call his name Immanuel (which means, God with us). Matthew 1:23

Question: Why do we call him Jesus?
Answer: **Jesus means Savior**. Jesus came to be the Savior of the world.

And we have seen and testify that the Father has sent his Son to be the Savior of the world. 1 John 4:14

Question: Why do we call him Christ?
Answer: **Christ means King.** Jesus came to be the King of Kings

On his robe and on his thigh he has a name written, King of kings and Lord of lords. Revelation 19:16

Question: Why do we call him Lord?
Answer: **Lord means God.** We should worship Jesus and give him honor and praise.

Thomas answered him, "My Lord and my God!" John 20:28

Question: Why did God send his Son to us?
Answer: **Jesus came to save sinners like me.** Through Jesus, God reveals his grace and glory.

"For the Son of Man came to seek and to save the lost." Luke 19:10

Question: What did Jesus do on earth?
Answer: **He lived a perfect life without sin**. Jesus did miracles and taught us about his kingdom.

You know that he appeared in order to take away sins, and in him there is no sin. 1 John 3:5

Question: Who were Jesus' disciples?
Answer: **Men and women who believed in him**. Disciples are those who follow Jesus.

Whoever does not bear his own cross and come after me cannot be my disciple. Luke 14:27

Question: Why did Jesus choose to die for us?
Answer: **To save us from our sins**. Jesus became our substitute sacrifice on the cross.

For our sake he made him to be sin who knew no sin, so that in him we might become the righteousness of God. 2 Corinthians 5:21

Part Three: Jesus Christ

30. Question: What happened after he died?

Answer: **He was wrapped in cloths and placed in a tomb**. It was a new tomb that belonged to a man named Joseph.

And Joseph took the body and wrapped it in a clean linen shroud and laid it in his own new tomb. Matthew 27:59-60

31. Question: Did Jesus remain dead?

Answer: **No, on the third day he came back to life**. His body was completely resurrected.

But the angel said to the women, "Do not be afraid, for I know that you seek Jesus who was crucified. He is not here, for he has risen. Matthew 28:5-6

32. Question: Did anyone see him after he rose from the dead?

Answer: **Yes, his disciples saw him**. Jesus remained with his disciples for another forty days and hundreds of people saw him.

He appeared to Cephas, then to the twelve. Then he appeared to more than five hundred brothers at one time. 1 Corinthians 15:5-6

33. Question: Where is the Lord Jesus Christ now?

Answer: **He went back to heaven to be with his Father.** Jesus Christ is ruling his kingdom from heaven until he returns to earth.

So then the Lord Jesus, after he had spoken to them, was taken up into heaven and sat down at the right hand of God. Mark 16:19

PART FOUR
THE HOLY SPIRIT

Question: Who is the Holy Spirit?

Answer: **The Holy Spirit is third person in the Trinity**. He is fully God just like God the Father and God the Son.

Go therefore and make disciples of all nations, baptizing them in the name of the Father and of the Son and of the Holy Spirit. Matthew 28:19

Question: Who sent the Holy Spirit to us?

Answer: **Jesus sent the Holy Spirit after he returned to heaven.** The Holy Spirit came down on the Day of Pentecost.

But the Helper, the Holy Spirit, whom the Father will send in my name, he will teach you all things and bring to your remembrance all that I have said to you. John 14:26

Question: Why did the Holy Spirit come to us?

Answer: **To convict people of their sin and guide them to the truth**. The Holy Spirit declares Gods truth in our hearts.

And when he comes, he will convict the world concerning sin and righteousness and judgment. John 16:8

Question: What does the Holy Spirit do?

Answer: **He gives witness to the truth about Jesus**. The Holy Spirit also bears witness that all who believe are God's children.

The Spirit himself bears witness with our spirit that we are children of God. Romans 8:16

Question: What is the New Covenant?

Answer: **The law of God written in our hearts by the Holy Spirit**. The New Covenant is offered to us through the body and blood of Jesus.

I will put my law within them, and I will write it on their hearts. And I will be their God, and they shall be my people. Jeremiah 31:33

 Question: How do you receive the Holy Spirit?

Answer: **By believing in Jesus**. When we trust Jesus for salvation, the Spirit lives in us and we become his temple.

Do you not know that you are God's temple and that God's Spirit dwells in you? 1 Corinthians 3:16

 Question: How does the Holy Spirit help Christians?

Answer: **He helps in our weakness to avoid sin**. The Holy Spirit also gave us the Bible so we can know and obey God.

The Spirit helps us in our weakness. For we do not know what to pray for as we ought, but the Spirit himself intercedes for us with groanings too deep for words. Romans 8:26

 Question: What gifts does the Holy Spirit give us?

Answer: **The fruit of the Spirit so we can walk in the Spirit**. The Holy Spirit also gives gifts to help the church.

But the fruit of the Spirit is love, joy, peace, patience, kindness, goodness, faithfulness, gentleness, self-control. Galatians 5:22–23

PART FIVE
CREATION AND PEOPLE

Part Five: Creation and People

Question: What is Creation?

Answer: **Creation is everything God made.** Everything that exists God made from nothing.

In the beginning, God created the heavens and the earth. Genesis 1:1

Question: How did God make everything?

Answer: **God spoke, and the universe began.** God made everything by his power and for his glory.

It is he who made the earth by his power, who established the world by his wisdom, and by his understanding stretched out the heavens. Jeremiah 51:15

Question: Did God make heaven too?

Answer: **Yes, he made heaven for himself and hell for the Devil.** God made everything we can see and everything we cannot see.

For by him all things were created, in heaven and on earth, visible and invisible, whether thrones or dominions or rulers or authorities. Colossians 1:16

Question: Who did God make first?

Answer: **God first made a man called Adam, then he made a woman called Eve.** They were both made in God's image.

So God created man in his own image, in the image of God he created him; male and female he created them. Genesis 1:27

 **Question: How did God make Adam and Eve?**

Answer: **God made Adam from the earth and made Eve from Adam.** They became our first parents.

For he knows our frame; he remembers that we are dust. Psalm 103:14

 Question: Did God make Adam and Eve different?

Answer: **Yes, God made Adam a man and Eve a woman.** In marriage, the man is the head of his wife and the woman is the helper of her husband.

For the husband is the head of the wife even as Christ is the head of the church, his body, and is himself its Savior. Ephesians 5:23

 Question: What did God give Adam and Eve besides bodies?

Answer: **God gave them spirits.** Our souls can never die.

Thus it is written, "The first man Adam became a living being"; the last Adam became a life giving spirit. 1 Corinthians 15:45

 Question: What were Adam and Eve like when God made them?

Answer: **They were holy and happy.** They were innocent before the Lord.

And the man and his wife were both naked and were not ashamed. Genesis 2:24

Part Five: Creation and People

 Question: What did God command Adam and Eve to do?

Answer: **God told them to be married and fill the earth with children**. Every human person comes from Adam and Eve.

And God blessed them. And God said to them, "Be fruitful and multiply and fill the earth and subdue it. Genesis 1:28a

 Question: When does a person's life begin?

Answer: **Like Jesus, a person's life begins at conception**. A person becomes a human being the moment they are conceived.

For you formed my inward parts; you knitted me together in my mother's womb. I praise you, for I am fearfully and wonderfully made. Psalm 139:13–14

 Question: Are people with a different skin color just like me?

Answer: **Yes, God makes people in many different colors**. All people are made in God's image and deserve our love and respect.

There is neither Jew nor Greek, there is neither slave nor free, there is no male and female, for you are all one in Christ Jesus. Galatians 3:28

Question: What else did God command Adam and Eve to do?

Answer: **God told them to take care of every plant and animal**. We are to be good stewards of God's creation.

And have dominion over the fish of the sea and over the birds of the heavens and over every living thing that moves on the earth. Genesis 1:28b

 Question: What did God do after he made everything?

Answer: **He said everything is very good and then he rested**. The sabbath is God's perfect peace and rest.

So God blessed the seventh day and made it holy, because on it God rested from all his work that he had done in creation. Genesis 2:3

PART SIX
THE FALL AND SIN

Part Six: The Fall and Sin

Question: Did Adam and Eve remain holy and happy?

Answer: **No. They sinned against the Lord.** They lost their innocence while in the Garden of Eden.

But like Adam they transgressed the covenant; there they dealt faithlessly with me.
Hosea 6:7

Question: What did they do wrong?

Answer: **They disobeyed by eating the forbidden fruit.** This was the first sin.

She took of its fruit and ate, and she also gave some to her husband who was with her, and he ate. Genesis 3:6

Question: How did this happen?

Answer: **Satan tempted Eve then she gave the fruit to Adam.** They were deceived by the Serpent.

But I am afraid that as the serpent deceived Eve by his cunning, your thoughts will be led astray from a sincere and pure devotion to Christ.
2 Corinthians 11:3

Question: What kind of punishment was given to Adam and Eve?

Answer: **They became sinners and death entered the world.** We call this the Fall.

For the wages of sin is death, but the free gift of God is eternal life in Christ Jesus our Lord.
Romans 6:23

Question: What did Adam's sin do to his children?

Answer: **We are all born into sin.** Everyone has a sin nature except Jesus.

Behold, I was brought forth in iniquity, and in sin did my mother conceive me. Psalm 51:5

 ### Question: What is sin?

Answer: **Sin is disobeying God.** It is thinking, saying or doing something that God does not like.

So whoever knows the right thing to do and fails to do it, for him it is sin. James 4:17

 ### Question: What does every sin deserve?

Answer: **Every sin deserves to be punished by God.** God's justice and righteousness demand judgment against sin.

For the wrath of God is revealed from heaven against all ungodliness and unrighteousness of men. Romans 1:18

 ### Question: Do we know how to obey God and avoid punishment?

Answer: **Yes, God has given us his law to obey.** He has written it in our hearts and in the Bible.

I will put my laws into their minds, and write them on their hearts. Hebrews 8:10

PART SEVEN
GOD'S HOLY LAW

Part Seven: God's Holy Law

 Question: What is the purpose of God's Law?

Answer: **To be holy like God**. God's children are to be holy like their Heavenly Father.

Speak to all the congregation of the people of Israel and say to them, You shall be holy, for I the Lord your God am holy. Leviticus 19:2

 Question: What are the greatest commands in the Law?

Answer: **There are two: Love God and love your neighbor**. Jesus told us these two are the Greatest of commands.

And Jesus said to him, "You shall love the Lord your God with all your heart and with all your soul and with all your mind. This is the great and first commandment. And a second is like it: You shall love your neighbor as yourself. Matthew 22:37–39

 Question: How many commandments did God give Moses on Mt. Sinai?

Answer: **God wrote ten commandments on stone tablets**. He gave Moses many other laws, but they are summarized in the Ten Commandments.

The Lord said to Moses, "Come up to me on the mountain and wait there, that I may give you the tablets of stone, with the law and the commandment, which I have written for their instruction. Exodus 24:12

66 Question: What is the first commandment?

Answer: **"You shall have no other gods before me."** We must only worship God.

Then Jesus said to him, "Be gone, Satan! For it is written, 'You shall worship the Lord your God and him only shall you serve.'" Matthew 4:10

67 Question: What is the second commandment?

Answer: **"You shall not make for yourself an idol."** We must worship the Lord in our hearts and not worship anything we make with our hands.

You shall not make for yourself a carved image, or any likeness of anything that is in heaven above, or that is in the earth beneath, or that is in the water under the earth. Exodus 20:4

68 Question: What is the third commandment?

Answer: **"You shall not misuse the name of the Lord your God."** We must remember how great and holy God is when we speak his name.

You shall not take the name of the Lord your God in vain, for the Lord will not hold him guiltless who takes his name in vain. Exodus 20:7

Part Seven: God's Holy Law

 Question: What is the fourth commandment?

Answer: **"Remember the Sabbath day by keeping it holy."** We must take time to rest from work and worship the Lord with God's people.

*Six days you shall labor, and do all your work, but the seventh day is a Sabbath to the L*ORD *your God. Exodus 20:9*

 Question: What day of the week do most Christians gather as a church to worship?

Answer: **On Sunday and we call it the Lord's Day**. It was on Sunday that Jesus rose from the dead and the first church came together to worship on Sunday.

But on the first day of the week, at early dawn, they went to the tomb, taking the spices they had prepared. And they found the stone rolled away from the tomb. Luke 24:1-2

 Question: What is the fifth commandment?

Answer: **"Honor your father and your mother."** God gave us parents to love and obey just like we love and obey him.

Children, obey your parents in everything, for this pleases the Lord. Colossians 3:20

Question: What is the sixth commandment?

Answer: **"You shall not murder."** We must love people and not want them to be harmed.

Everyone who hates his brother is a murderer, and you know that no murderer has eternal life abiding in him. 1 John 3:15

 Question: What is the seventh commandment?

Answer: **"You shall not commit adultery."** We must keep our hearts and our marriages pure before the Lord.

For you may be sure of this, that everyone who is sexually immoral or impure, or who is covetous (that is, an idolater), has no inheritance in the kingdom of Christ and God. Ephesians 5:5

 Question: What is the eighth commandment?

Answer: **"You shall not steal."** We must not take things that belong to others and we should share with others the things God has given us.

Let the thief no longer steal, but rather let him labor, doing honest work with his own hands, so that he may have something to share with anyone in need. Ephesians 4:28

Part Seven: God's Holy Law

 Question: What is the ninth commandment?

Answer: **"You shall not tell lies."** We must always tell the truth and never say anything that would hurt another person.

Therefore, having put away falsehood, let each one of you speak the truth with his neighbor, for we are members one of another. Ephesians 4:25

 Question: What is the tenth commandment?

Answer: **"You shall not covet."** We must not be jealous for things other people have and always be content with the things God has given us.

Keep your life free from love of money, and be content with what you have, for he has said, "I will never leave you nor forsake you."
Hebrews 13:5

 Question: Can anyone keep all these commandments?

Answer: **No one can except for Jesus.** Because of our sin nature, we are not able to be holy like God is, but Jesus never sinned and always remained holy.

For we do not have a high priest who is unable to sympathize with our weaknesses, but one who in every respect has been tempted as we are, yet without sin. Hebrews 4:15

Question: What can learn from Gods' law and commandments?

Answer: **They teach us about God's holiness and reveal our sinfulness**. God's law is good and it helps us to see our need for a Savior.

For by works of the law no human being will be justified in his sight, since through the law comes knowledge of sin. Romans 3:20

 ### Question: Will God condemn us for not obeying his law?

Answer: **Yes, unless we repent of our sins and place faith in Jesus**. God sent his Son Jesus to fulfill the law for us and die on a cross to save us.

So then, the law was our guardian until Christ came, in order that we might be justified by faith. Galatians 3:24

PART EIGHT
SALVATION

Part Eight: Salvation

Question: What is the gospel?

Answer: **The gospel is the good news about Jesus**. Christ died on a cross, was buried, and rose again for our salvation.

For I am not ashamed of the gospel, for it is the power of God for salvation to everyone who believes, to the Jew first and also to the Greek. Romans 1:16

Question: Why did Jesus have to die on a cross?

Answer: **Jesus died because God must punish sin**. On the cross Christ paid for all my sin through his shed blood.

In this is love, not that we have loved God but that he loved us and sent his Son to be the propitiation for our sins. 1 John 4:10

Question: Why did Jesus have to rise from the dead?

Answer: **Jesus rose from the grave to defeat death**. The resurrection proves Christ's victory over sin and gives us hope.

*The sting of death is sin, and the power of sin is the law. But thanks be to God, who gives us the victory through our Lord Jesus Christ.
1 Corinthians 15:56–57*

Question: What is salvation?

Answer: **When God rescues people from their sins**. In salvation, God delivers me from the consequences of my sin and rescues me from hell.

He has delivered us from the domain of darkness and transferred us to the kingdom of his beloved Son, in whom we have redemption, the forgiveness of sins. Colossians 1:13-14

Question: What is grace?

Answer: **Grace is God's loving favor upon the unlovely**. Salvation is a gift of God's grace and not something we deserve because of our good works.

For by grace you have been saved through faith. And this is not your own doing; it is the gift of God, not a result of works, so that no one may boast. Ephesians 2:8-10

Question: What is repentance?

Answer: **Being sorry for my sin against God**. Repentance means I hate my sin like God hates it so I stop sinning.

For godly grief produces a repentance that leads to salvation without regret, whereas worldly grief produces death. 2 Corinthians 7:10

Part Eight: Salvation

 Question: What does it mean to be "born again"?

Answer: **Our hearts are made alive by the Holy Spirit**. Regeneration is a change of heart that leads a person to repent and place faith in Jesus for salvation.

Jesus answered, "Truly, truly, I say to you, unless one is born of water and the Spirit, he cannot enter the kingdom of God. John 3:5

 Question: What is election?

Answer: **God's loving choice for many sinners to be saved**. God's election is based upon his goodness and mercy and not in any good he sees in us.

He chose us in him before the foundation of the world, that we should be holy and blameless before him. Ephesians 1:4

 Question: What is justification?

Answer: **God declares us not guilty of our sins**. We are justified by faith in Christ alone and we also receive Christ's righteousness that covers our unrighteousness.

Therefore, since we have been justified by faith, we have peace with God through our Lord Jesus Christ. Romans 5:1

 Question: What is adoption?

Answer: **God makes us members of his family**. Through adoption we enjoy all the privileges of being God's children.

In love he predestined us for adoption to himself as sons through Jesus Christ, according to the purpose of his will. Ephesians 1:5

Question: What is sanctification?

Answer: **God makes us holy like himself.** Through sanctification, the Holy Spirit makes us more and more like Christ.

But now that you have been set free from sin and have become slaves of God, the fruit you get leads to sanctification and its end, eternal life. Romans 6:22

 Question: What is glorification?

Answer: **When Jesus returns, we will be like him.** Glorification is the final step in salvation where believers will live in their resurrected bodies forever with the Lord.

And those whom he predestined he also called, and those whom he called he also justified, and those whom he justified he also glorified. Romans 8:30

 Question: Can salvation be lost?

Answer: **Nothing can take away God's salvation.** The Holy Spirit seals every believer and gives them power to persevere.

And I am sure of this, that he who began a good work in you will bring it to completion at the day of Jesus Christ. Philippians 1:6

PART NINE
PRAYER

Part Nine: Prayer

Question: What is prayer?
Answer: **Prayer is talking to God**. When we pray we give God thanks and share our concerns with him.

Do not be anxious about anything, but in everything by prayer and supplication with thanksgiving let your requests be made known to God.
Philippians 4:6

Question: Why should we pray?
Answer: **Because God wants to hear our prayers**. It pleases God when we call upon him.

Then you will call upon me and come and pray to me, and I will hear you. You will seek me and find me, when you seek me with all your heart.
Jeremiah 29:12–13

Question: When should we pray?
Answer: **We should pray often**. There are many times each day that we should thank God and ask for his help.

Rejoice always, pray without ceasing, give thanks in all circumstances; for this is the will of God in Christ Jesus for you.
1 Thessalonians 5:16–18

Question: How should we pray?
Answer: **We should pray by faith in Jesus name**. Christ helps to bring our prayers before the Heavenly Father.

Truly, truly, I say to you, whatever you ask of the Father in my name, he will give it to you.
John 16:23

Question: Who should we pray for?

Answer: **We should pray for everyone**. We should pray for our family, our friends, our leaders, those who are sick, and for lost people to be saved.

First of all, then, I urge that supplications, prayers, intercessions, and thanksgivings be made for all people. 1 Timothy 2:1

 Question: What should we pray for?

Answer: **We should pray for God's will to be done**. We should ask God for things that will bring him glory.

And this is the confidence that we have toward him, that if we ask anything according to his will he hears us. 1 John 5:14

 Question: Did Jesus pray?

Answer: **Yes, Jesus taught us how to pray**. We call this the Lord's prayer.

Our Father in heaven, hallowed be your name. Your kingdom come, your will be done, on earth as it is in heaven. Give us this day our daily bread, and forgive us our debts, as we also have forgiven our debtors. And lead us not into temptation, but deliver us from evil. Matthew 6:9-13

PART TEN
THE CHURCH

Part Ten: The Church

Question: What is the Church?
Answer: **The body of Christ**. Jesus purchased the church with his shed blood on the cross.

So we, though many, are one body in Christ, and individually members one of another.
Romans 12:5

Question: Who is the head of the church?
Answer: **Jesus is the head of his church**. Only people who believe in Christ become a part of his body.

For the husband is the head of the wife even as Christ is the head of the church, his body, and is himself its Savior.
Ephesians 5:23

Question: What is the local church?
Answer: **Where Christians gather to worship**. Members of local churches come together for preaching, fellowship, prayer, and to celebrate the ordinances.

And they devoted themselves to the apostles' teaching and the fellowship, to the breaking of bread and the prayers.
Acts 2:42

Question: How often should the church meet to worship?

Answer: **The church should meet every week**. It is important to come to church so we can encourage each other to love and obey God.

And let us consider how to stir up one another to love and good works, not neglecting to meet together, as is the habit of some, but encouraging one another Hebrews 10:24-25

Question: What is the mission of the church?

Answer: **To make disciples everywhere**. We are to share the gospel with everyone and start new churches all over the world.

Go therefore and make disciples of all nations, baptizing them in the name of the Father and of the Son and of the Holy Spirit, teaching them to observe all that I have commanded you. Matthew 28:19-20

Question: Who are the leaders of the church?

Answer: **Jesus gives pastors to lead his church**. Pastors or Elders are in charge of the church and deacons are to help them serve the members of the church.

To all the saints in Christ Jesus who are at Philippi, with the overseers and deacons. Philippians 1:1

Part Ten: The Church

 Question: What ordinances did Jesus give to local churches?

Answer: **Believer's Baptism and the Lord's Supper**. Baptism shows that we belong to Christ and the Lord's Supper reminds us what he did for us on the cross.

So those who received his word were baptized, and there were added that day about three thousand souls. Acts 2:41

On the first day of the week, when we were gathered together to break bread, Paul talked with them. Acts 20:7

 Question: What is baptism?

Answer: **When a Christian is dipped into water**. It is a public confession to show a person has identified with Christ's death, burial, and resurrection.

We were buried therefore with him by baptism into death, in order that, just as Christ was raised from the dead by the glory of the Father, we too might walk in newness of life. Romans 6:4

 Question: Who should be baptized?

Answer: **All who repent and trust in Jesus**. Believer's baptism is one of the first acts of obedience for Christians.

*But when they believed Philip as he preached good news about the kingdom of God and the name of Jesus Christ, they were baptized, both men and women.
Acts 8:12*

109 Question: What is the Lord's Supper?

Answer: **A special meal the church enjoys.** Believers share the bread and the cup to remember the Lord's death until he returns.

For as often as you eat this bread and drink the cup, you proclaim the Lord's death until he comes. 1 Corinthians 11:26

110 Question: What does the bread and cup represent?

Answer: **The body and blood of Jesus.** Jesus body was given for us as a sacrifice and his blood was shed on the cross to remove our sins.

*And he took bread, and when he had given thanks, he broke it and gave it to them, saying, "This is my body, which is given for you. Do this in remembrance of me." And likewise the cup after they had eaten, saying, "This cup that is poured out for you is the new covenant in my blood.
Luke 22:19–20*

111 Question: Who should take the Lord's Supper?

Answer: **Everyone who is saved and baptized.** The Lord's Supper helps the church to maintain unity and purity.

Because there is one bread, we who are many are one body, for we all partake of the one bread. 1 Corinthians 10:17

Part Ten: The Church

 Question: What is the responsibility of church members?

Answer: **To love each another**. Church members should humbly serve, care, warn, and encourage one another.

Love one another with brotherly affection. Outdo one another in showing honor.
Romans 12:10

PART ELEVEN
ANGELS AND DEMONS

Part Eleven: Angels and Demons

Question: Did God make the angels?

Answer: **Yes, God made angels.** The Lord made everything that is visible and invisible.

You are the Lord, you alone. You have made heaven, the heaven of heavens, with all their host, the earth and all that is on it, the seas and all that is in them; and you preserve all of them; and the host of heaven worships you.
Nehemiah 9:6

Question: What are angels?

Answer: **They are powerful spirit creatures**. There are different types of angels, but they all exist to worship and serve the Lord.

And the four living creatures, each of them with six wings, are full of eyes all around and within, and day and night they never cease to say, "Holy, holy, holy, is the Lord God Almighty, who was and is and is to come!"
Revelation 4:8

Question: Where do angels live?

Answer: **Angels live in heaven**. Sometimes angels come to earth to protect and care for God's people.

For he will command his angels concerning you to guard you in all your ways.
Psalm 91:11

Question: How do angels serve God?

Answer: **They are God's messengers and protectors**. Angels announced the coming of Jesus and they will announce his glorious return.

And the angel said to them, "Fear not, for behold, I bring you good news of great joy that will be for all the people. For unto you is born this day in the city of David a Savior, who is Christ the Lord. Luke 2:10–11

Question: Did God make the Devil and demons too?

Answer: **Yes, but they were not bad at first**. The Devil became prideful and turned many angels away from God. They became evil demons.

You were blameless in your ways from the day you were created, till unrighteousness was found in you. Ezekiel 28:15

Question: Who is the Devil?

Answer: **The Devil is God's enemy**. He is a liar, a murderer, and a thief.

Be sober-minded; be watchful. Your adversary the devil prowls around like a roaring lion, seeking someone to devour. 1 Peter 5:8

Part Eleven: Angels and Demons

Question: What does the Devil do?

Answer: **The Devil deceives people**. He tempts people to believe lies.

He was a murderer from the beginning, and does not stand in the truth, because there is no truth in him. When he lies, he speaks out of his own character, for he is a liar and the father of lies. John 8:44

What are demons?

Answer: **Demons are fallen angels**. They serve their master Satan to harm us, but they are doomed for destruction.

*For we do not wrestle against flesh and blood, but against the rulers, against the authorities, against the cosmic powers over this present darkness, against the spiritual forces of evil in the heavenly places.
Ephesians 6:12*

Where do demons live?

Answer: **Demons live in hell**. Some demons come to earth to hurt people and do evil.

For if God did not spare angels when they sinned, but cast them into hell and committed them to chains of gloomy darkness to be kept until the judgment. 2 Peter 2:4

PART TWELVE
LAST THINGS

Question: What happens after the resurrection?

Answer: **He went back to heaven**. his place as King at the right hand of the Father.

But when Christ had offered for all time a single sacrifice for sins, he sat down at the right hand of God, waiting from that time until his enemies should be made a footstool for his feet. Hebrews 10:12–13

Question: Will Jesus come to earth again?

Answer: **Yes, he will come to judge the world**. At the second coming Christ will return to earth with angel armies to glorify his saints and condemn his enemies.

I charge you in the presence of God and of Christ Jesus, who is to judge the living and the dead, and by his appearing and his kingdom. 2 Timothy 4:1

Question: When will Jesus return to earth?

Answer: **Only God knows**. The Heavenly Father has chosen the time when his Son will return to the earth.

"But concerning that day and hour no one knows, not even the angels of heaven, nor the Son, but the Father only." Matthew 24:36

Question: What happens to unbelievers on the Day of Judgment?

Answer: **The Lord will throw them into hell**. They will suffer the consequences for every sin they committed against God.

And if anyone's name was not found written in the book of life, he was thrown into the lake of fire. Revelation 20:15

Question: What is hell?

Answer: **Hell is a place of punishment**. The Lake of Fire will be a place of eternal torment and suffering.

The Son of Man will send his angels, and they will gather out of his kingdom all causes of sin and all law-breakers, and throw them into the fiery furnace. In that place there will be weeping and gnashing of teeth. Matthew 13:41–42

Question: Does God wish for people to go to hell?

Answer: **No, God wants everyone to repent**. God's holiness and justice demands punishment for everyone who dies in their sin.

As I live, declares the Lord GOD, I have no pleasure in the death of the wicked, but that the wicked turn from his way and live; turn back, turn back from your evil ways. Ezekiel 33:11

Part Twelve: Last Things

Question: What happens to Christians when they die?

Answer: **Their bodies return to dust, but their spirits go to Jesus**. Their bodies have to wait until Jesus returns to glorify them.

Yes, we are of good courage, and we would rather be away from the body and at home with the Lord. 2 Corinthians 5:8

Question: What happens to Christians on Day of Judgment?

Answer: **They will live with Jesus forever**. All believers will be given rewards for their good deeds, but the ultimate prize is to be with Jesus.

"Behold, I am coming soon, bringing my recompense with me, to repay each one for what he has done." Revelation 22:12

Question: What is heaven?

Answer: **Heaven is Jesus' perfect home**. He is preparing places for all believers to live with him forever.

In my Father's house are many rooms. If it were not so, would I have told you that I go to prepare a place for you? John 14:2

Question: Will there be any sin in heaven?

Answer: **There will be no sin in heaven.** Everything in heaven will be perfect and complete, including every Christian.

He will wipe away every tear from their eyes, and death shall be no more, neither shall there be mourning, nor crying, nor pain anymore, for the former things have passed away. Revelation 21:4

 Question: What will we do in heaven?

Answer: **We will worship God and enjoy him forever.** In heaven, our desires will be to worship God, love each other, and enjoy the rewards we will be given.

No longer will there be anything accursed, but the throne of God and of the Lamb will be in it, and his servants will worship him. Revelation 22:3

 Question: How long will heaven and hell last?

Answer: **They both will last forever.** When Jesus returns, he will send believers to a new heaven and unbelievers will be cast into an eternal lake of fire.

And these will go away into eternal punishment, but the righteous into eternal life. Matthew 25:46

Part Twelve: Last Things

Question: Will God's truth in the Bible ever change?

Answer: **No, the Bible will never change because God cannot change**. None of the words in the Bible should ever be removed and no words should be added.

"And behold, I am coming soon. Blessed is the one who keeps the words of the prophecy of this book." Revelation 22:7

Question: What should I do now that I am finished with this catechism?

Answer: **Believe in Jesus and live for him**. I must continue to grow in the grace and knowledge of Jesus and the gospel.

But grow in the grace and knowledge of our Lord and Savior Jesus Christ. To him be the glory both now and to the day of eternity. Amen. 2 Peter 3:18

FINDING L.I.F.E. IN JESUS

Everyone wants to be happy. The hard part is determining exactly what that means. For some, happiness is defined through relationships. They believe that popularity, a huge friend list on Facebook, and a significant other produces happiness. For others, happiness is defined through success. They believe that personal achievement, a huge number in their bank account, and plenty of expensive toys produces happiness. For still others, happiness is defined through community. They believe that personal growth, a huge impact for societal change, and embracing diversity produces happiness. And these things do—until they don't.

Experiencing happiness is as difficult as catching the greased pig at the county fair. It appears to be right in front of us, but then it slips through our fingers and is gone. Friends, achievement, and personal growth have the potential to bring happiness into our lives, but when our friends disappear, success eludes us, and we realize that we're incapable of self-transformation, happiness is quickly replaced by disillusionment and depression. The problem with pursuing happiness is that it is an emotion that is driven by our circumstances. And let's be honest—we all tend to have more negative than positive experiences in our lives.

So, what's the answer? Should we keep doing the same things while expecting different results, or should we consider what Jesus has to say about finding our purpose for life? If you want to stay on the hamster wheel while you try to catch up to happiness, you can stop reading here. But if you're ready to consider what God wants to do in your life, please read on.

God never promises happiness in the Bible. Are you surprised to hear that? Instead, he promises something much greater—joy. While happiness is an emotion fueled by circumstance, joy is an attitude fueled by God's Spirit. Happiness is self-determined. In other words, I am the sole determiner of whether I'm happy at any given moment. Joy, on the other hand, is God-determined. God has promised to give us joy, and it isn't based on our circumstances—it's based on God's character and promises.

This is why Jesus never talks about giving people happiness. He knew all too well that chasing happiness is like chasing your shadow. You can never catch it. Instead, he talks about giving people life. He said, "I came that they may have life and have it abundantly (Jn 10:10)." Here, Jesus reveals that the thing people really want, whether they know it or not, is abundant life. To have an abundant life means that you are personally satisfied in all areas of your life, and you experience peace and contentment as a result. Jesus' statement also means that we do not have the capacity to create that kind of life for ourselves. Jesus came in order to give it to us. But how? The Bible tells us that achieving this kind of satisfied life requires us to know something about God, ourselves, and the reason for the death and resurrection of Jesus Christ.

First, we must understand God's **love**. The Bible says that God is love (I Jn 4:8), and God created us so that we could know him and experience his love (Gen 1:26-31). God created us to be worshipers and to live forever in the reality of his glory. And, when sin marred his perfect creation, he created a plan to free men and women from its curse. At just the right time in history, God sent his own Son, Jesus, into our world. "For God so loved the world, that he gave his only Son, that whoever believes in him should not perish but have eternal life (Jn 3:16)." It is God's love that motivates him to restore relationship with those who are separated from him by sin.

Second, we must understand our **isolation**. To be isolated is to be separated from someone, and as a result, to be alone. This is what sin has done to us. It has separated us from the very one we were created to know, love, and worship—God. When Adam and Eve rebelled against God by breaking the lone command he had given them, the entire world was brought under the curse of sin (Gen 3). As a result, God removed them from the Garden of Eden, and their perfect fellowship with God was broken. In an instant, they had become isolated from God because of their sin. From that moment to this, every person born into this world is guilty of sin. The Bible says, "For all have sinned and fall short of the glory of God (Rom 3:23)." Because of this "there is none righteous, no, not one (Rom 3:10)." Further, "The wages of sin is death (Rom 6:23a)." We were created to love and worship God in perfect community, but now because of sin we are isolated from him. Meanwhile, we try to satisfy this desire to know God by pursuing our own happiness, even though we can never hope to attain it. And in doing so, we risk being isolated from God for all eternity.

Third, we must understand our need for **forgiveness**. There is only one way to experience God's love and escape the isolation caused by sin—we must experience God's forgiveness. In spite of sin, God never stopped loving the people he created. He promised Adam and Eve that he would send someone who could fix the problem they had created. When it was time, God sent his own Son, Jesus, to be the world's Savior. This, too, was an act of God's love. The Bible says, "God shows his love for us in that while we were still sinners, Christ died for us (Rom 5:8)." When Jesus died on the cross, he was paying the penalty for our sins (Rom 3:23-26). When God raised Jesus from the dead, it was to demonstrate that forgiveness was available to all who would receive it by faith. Paul explained how this happens in his letter to the Ephesians. "For by grace you have been saved through faith. And this is not your own doing; it is the gift of God, not a result of works, so that no one may boast (Eph 2:8-9)."

The reality is that we cannot experience salvation as a result of our own efforts. We can try to be a good person, go to a church, even give a ton of money to worthy causes—none of these "works" can provide forgiveness. No matter how hard we try, we will always "fall short of the glory of God." That is why we must receive God's offer of forgiveness and salvation by faith. Faith simply means to trust or believe. Salvation requires us to believe that God loves us, that we are isolated from him by our sins, and that his Son Jesus died and was raised to life again to pay the sin debt that we owe God because of our sins. When we take God up on his offer of the gift of salvation, he doesn't just give us forgiveness—he gives us life! The Bible says, "The free gift of God is eternal life in Christ Jesus our Lord (Rom 6:23)."

Fourth, we must understand the **enjoyment** that comes from knowing, loving, and worshiping God. Whether we know it or not, we are slaves to sin until God sets us free (Rom 6:20-23). This was the ultimate reason that God sent his Son, Jesus, to die on the cross for our sins—God sent Jesus so that we could be set free from our sins. Jesus said, "You will know the truth, and the truth will set you free. . . .Everyone who commits sin is a slave to sin. . . .So, if the Son sets you free, you will be free indeed (Jn 8:32-36)." Jesus was teaching us that we must be set free from sin in order to enjoy the life that God has given us—both now and in eternity future. We are set free when we commit our lives to Jesus Christ through faith in his death and resurrection. Then, and only then, will we find joy in the abundant life of Jesus Christ!

So, the question for you is a simple one: Are you ready to experience freedom from sin and the abundant life that Jesus promised you? If so, God is waiting for to talk with him about it (Jer 29:13). Stop right where you are and make this your prayer to God,

> "Father in heaven, I know that I'm a sinner. I know that I've done lots of things that displease you and disappoint you. And, I know that I'm isolated from you because of my sin. I know that if I die without knowing you, I will spend forever separated from you in hell. But, I believe that Jesus is your sinless Son, and I believe that he died on the cross for me. I believe that he died to provide a perfect payment for my sin debt. I believe that you raised him from the dead so that I could experience forgiveness for my sins. Right now, Father, I'm asking you to forgive me of my sins and save me. I am receiving your Son Jesus as my personal Lord and Savior. I will follow you the rest of my life. Please give me the joy of a life spent knowing, loving, and worshiping you. I ask these things in Jesus' name, Amen."

If you made the decision to accept Jesus as your Savior today, we want to talk with you! Please contact the people at www.seed-publishing-group.com. We would love to talk with you about your decision and help you with your first steps in following Jesus!

Check out other books from Seed Publishing Group!

30 DAYS TO JAMES
FOREWORD BY DR. TONY MERIDA
A DEVOTIONAL COMMENTARY
BILL CURTIS

30 DAYS TO ACTS
FOREWORD BY DR. JOHN AVANT
A DEVOTIONAL COMMENTARY
DOUG MUNTON

30 DAYS TO GENESIS
FOREWORD BY DR. ED HINDSON
A DEVOTIONAL COMMENTARY
CHET RODEN

30 DAYS TO RUTH/ESTHER
PORTRAITS OF PROVIDENCE
A DEVOTIONAL COMMENTARY
LYLA CURTIS

All titles are available on Amazon.

Made in United States
North Haven, CT
12 January 2022